BY VALERIE BODDEN

CREATIVE EDUCATION

Published by Creative Education
P.O. Box 227, Mankato, Minnesota 56002
Creative Education is an imprint of The Creative Company
www.thecreativecompany.us

Design and production by The Design Lab
Art direction by Rita Marshall
Printed in the United States of America

Photographs by Corbis (Robert Holmes, Hulton-Deutsch
Collection, Didrik Johnck, David Keaton, Teru Kuwayama,
Joe McDonald, Warren Morgan, Douglas Peebles, Galen
Rowell, John Van Hasselt), iStockphoto (Stuart Murchison),
Jake Norton/Mountain World Photography

Library of Congress Cataloging-in-Publication Data
Bodden, Valerie.
Mount Everest / by Valerie Bodden.
p. cm. — (Big outdoors)
Summary: A fundamental introduction to Mount Everest, including
the snowy forests that surround it, the creatures that live near it,
and how people have affected its high-altitude environment.
Includes index.
ISBN 978-1-58341-817-8
1. Everest, Mount (China and Nepal)—
Juvenile literature. I. Title. II. Series.

DS495.8.E9B63 2010
954.96—dc22   2009004690

First Edition
9 8 7 6 5 4 3 2 1

MOUNT EVEREST

ASIA
★

Mount Everest (*EV-er-ist*) is the tallest **mountain** in the world. It is on the **continent** of Asia. Half of the mountain is in the country of Nepal. Half is in an area of China called Tibet. Mount Everest is part of the Himalayan (*him-uh-LAY-en*) mountains.

Mount Everest (center of photo) can be seen from outer space

Some people in Nepal
call Mount Everest "The
Forehead of the Sky."

Mount Everest is 29,035 feet (8,850 m) tall. That's as high as jets fly in the sky! Mount Everest has three sides. The sides are shaped like triangles.

Most of Everest is made of a dark rock called gneiss (*NEES*)

Scientists think that Mount Everest was formed a long time ago. They think that two **plates** of the earth's **crust** crashed into each other. The crash pushed up a lot of rock and made the Himalayas.

The Himalayas were shaped by ice (above) and lava (opposite)

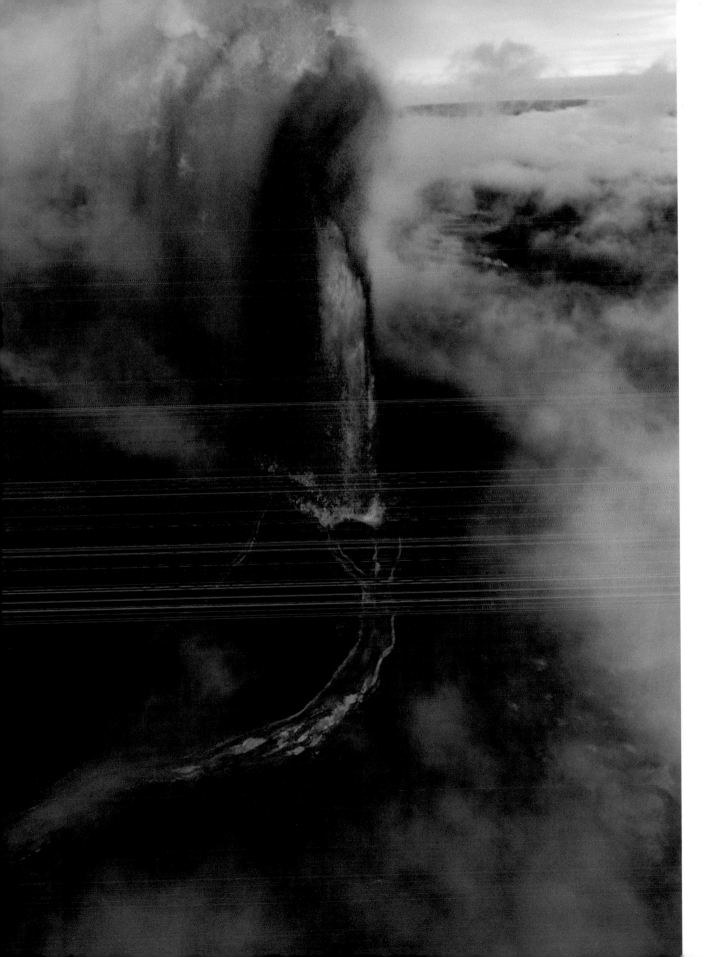

Many Sherpas work as guides to lead climbers up Mount Everest.

The weather on Mount Everest is very cold, even in the summer. It is covered with snow year-round. People do not live on Mount Everest. But people called Sherpas live in villages near the bottom of the mountain.

Climbers travel through villages in Nepal to reach Mount Everest

Forests of pine and hemlock trees grow at the bottom of Mount Everest. Musk deer and Himalayan tahrs (*TARZ*) live there. Himalayan tahrs look like goats.

Animals like pikas (above) and tahrs (opposite) live on Everest

Higher up on the mountain, there are no trees. But there are **shrubs**. Snow leopards and mountain sheep climb in these areas. Nothing lives at the very top of Mount Everest.

Snow leopards (opposite) can survive well on the rocky mountain

About 50 years ago, the first people climbed to the top of Mount Everest. Their names were Edmund Hillary and Tenzing Norgay. Since then, more than 1,200 people have reached the top.

People celebrated Tenzing Norgay and Edmund Hillary's climb

A Sherpa named Appa has climbed Mount Everest more than 15 times!

More than 175 people
have died trying to
climb Mount Everest.

In the past, many climbers left garbage on Mount Everest. Some people cut down trees for firewood. But today, leaders in Nepal and Tibet are making sure people take better care of the mountain.

Visitors to Everest have left their marks on some of the rocks

Every year, hundreds of people try to climb Mount Everest. It can take them more than two months to reach the top. But when they get there, they can enjoy the view from "the roof of the world"!

A ladder bridge (above) can help climbers get to the top (opposite)

Climbers use ropes and ladder bridges to help them get up Mount Everest.

People in the Himalayas use yaks to carry their things up mountains.

Glossary

continent one of Earth's seven big pieces of land

crust the solid top layer of the earth that makes up the ground people walk on

mountain a very tall, steep hill made out of rock

plates parts of Earth's crust that move together; when plates move, it can cause earthquakes

shrubs short, woody plants that have many stems

yaks large, buffalo-like animals with long hair and curved horns

Read More about It

Castelain, Celine. *Asha: A Child of the Himalayas*. Farmington Hills, Mich.: Blackbirch Press, 2005.

De Capua, Sarah. *Mount Everest*. New York: Children's Press, 2002.

Index